Gold Medal Advisory Board

Gregory Smith
Editor in Chief/Skating Magazine
United States Figure Skating Association

Carol Heiss Jenkins
Gold Medalist 1960
Television Commentator/Teacher

Robert Purdy
Executive Director
A.A.U. Bobsledding Association

Thomas E. Hall
Executive Director
Ice Skating Institute
of America

Col. F. Donald Miller
Executive Director
United States
Olympic Committee

William Markland
Board of Directors/
United States International
Speed Skating Association

William D. Traeger
Executive Director
United States Ski Team

Larry Ralston
Permanent Secretary
American Skating Union

Dick Button
Gold Medalist 1948-52
Television Producer/Commentator

Hal Trumble
Executive Director
United States Amateur Hockey Association

Diane Holum
Gold Medalist 1972
Coach/United States Olympic
Speed skating team

George Howie
National Director
United States International Speed Skating Association

OLYMPIC ALPINE SKIING

By the staff of the Ice Skating Institute of America
in cooperation with the United States Olympic Committee

CHILDRENS PRESS, CHICAGO

A downhill racer turns between the flags.

Photographs in this book courtesy of the Ice Skating Institute of America, publisher, *XIII Olympic Winter Games, Lake Placid,* © 1979.
Created by T.A. Chacharon & Assoc. Ltd.

Cover photograph: An Olympic skier on his way down a course.
Page 1 photograph: The beautiful Sapporo, Japan Alpine skiing course.

LIBRARY OF CONGRESS CATALOGING IN PUBLICATION DATA

Ice Skating Institute of America
Olympic Alpine skiing.

SUMMARY: Discusses the origins, equipment, techniques, and events of Olympic Alpine skiing and highlights the achievements of several Olympic champions.
1. Ski racing—Juvenile literature. 2. Skiers—Biography—Juvenile literature. 3. Olympic games—Juvenile literature. [1. Ski racing. 2. Skiers. 3. Olympic games (winter)] I. United States Olympic Committee. II. Title.
GV854.9.R3I24 1979 796.9'3 79-19029
ISBN 0-516-02551-1

You stand at the top of the world. On every side of you are mountains. But you do not see the mountains or the beautiful blue sky above them. You have a purpose, a goal. Now is the time to reach that goal. You stand in the starting gate. This will be one of the most important races of your life.

The signal is given: Go! You fly into action, using your poles and your legs to push you down the course that is laid out before you. You move back and forth, now leaning forward to go faster, now leaning sideways to cut across the mountainside. In front of you is whiteness; flashing by you are trees and brightly clothed crowds of people.

You hear your time being called out. You must go faster! Every muscle of your body is involved in hurtling down the mountain. You slice the snow with your turns. You waste no motion. You see nothing but the snow and the flags you must pass.

Ahead is the end of the course. No turning or maneuvering possible now. Only speed. Every ounce of your strength is used for these final moments. You pass through the last gate, come to a quick stop, and immediately turn to the scoreboard. There is a minute of unbearable suspense. Then your time flashes on the scoreboard. You have won—not only against the other skiers, but against yourself and the limitations of your body. You are an Olympic champion!

Until the mid-1800s the only skiing done was cross-country, or Nordic skiing. Skis were used for travel over snow-covered level ground or small hills only, as this type of ski could not be controlled on steep skiing surfaces. Alpine skiing was developed in the late 1800s. The new type of ski and ski boot made it possible for skiers to ski on steep surfaces.

Olympic Alpine skiing is fascinating to watch. The skiers are racing against time on slippery and sometimes treacherous snow. This kind of skiing combines the grace and strength of a superb athlete, the beauty of mountains and forest, and the overcoming of physical limitations in a brief, wonderful battle. Those who watch and those who ski in these races can almost believe that man can indeed fly.

HOW ALPINE RACING BEGAN

Skiing is a very old art. People have been using skis for more than 4,000 years. Skiing was not thought of as a sport, however, until the mid-1800s. All the skiing done until that time was cross-country, or Nordic, skiing. The skis used for cross-country were good only for traveling over level ground or small hills. A skier could not control a cross-country ski on steep skiing surfaces, because only the toe of the skiing boot was attached to the ski.

When new ways to attach the ski boot more firmly to the ski were developed, it became possible for skiers to ski down a mountainside. British tourists vacationing in the Alps of Europe began to ski on mountain slopes. The idea caught on, and soon many skiing techniques were developed. The earliest kind of race was the downhill race, first held in 1893. Different kinds of turns were invented. Then came the slalom (SLAH-lum) race, in which skiers followed a twisting course instead of a straight one. The first slalom race was held in 1923.

Opposite: Whiteface Mountain, in Lake Placid, New York, will offer many challenges for Alpine skiers.

Since the sport was becoming more popular, an organization was formed to set up rules for skiing events. This was the Federation Internationale de Ski (FIS). Skiing became even more popular when ski lifts were built at ski resorts. Before then, skiers had to trudge up a mountain, put on their skis, and ski back down. Soon skiers began asking for the recognition of Alpine skiing as a separate sport from Nordic skiing. The first world championships for Alpine downhill and slalom races were held in 1931. These two events were added to the Olympics in 1936. Alpine skiing had become a sport in its own right. One more event was to come—the giant slalom. The first such race was held in 1949, and it joined the other two Alpine events in the 1952 Olympics.

An amazing amount of progress has been made in perfecting ski equipment and techniques in the short length of time skiing has been popular. As interest in Alpine skiing grew, methods of skiing faster, more safely, and in better control were developed. Today it is a very popular pastime, and one of the most exciting of Olympic competitions.

Alpine skis used in races are lightweight; the front and back ends are turned up so they will not catch in the snow. Here, Cindy Nelson of the United States uses the sharp metal edges of her skis for control on a difficult downhill turn during her race for a bronze medal at Innsbruck, Austria in 1976.

SKIS AND SKIING EQUIPMENT

Many kinds of skis are made for Alpine skiing. All are made with the front and back ends turned up so they will not catch in the snow. They are fairly lightweight. Alpine skis used in races have sharp metal edges on both sides. These edges bite into snow and ice, and give skiers greater control when they turn. An Alpine ski also has a groove on the bottom that runs down the length of the ski. This groove helps the skier move in a straight line. The materials used in making skis include wood, metal, and fiberglass. Each ski is slightly arched in the center. This arch is called the *camber.* The camber gives the ski some spring. This helps skiers when shifting their body weight to maneuver down a slope.

There are different kinds of skis for each racing event. Downhill skis are flexible in the front so they will go over bumps in the snow easily. They have a stiff back end, or *tail,* which helps the skier ski in a straight line. They are the longest and most stable of the racing skis. Slalom skis are shorter than downhill skis. They have a stiff front end and camber, but a more flexible tail. This kind of tail helps skiers control their skis on turns. The ski used for the giant slalom is between the other two in length. With it the racer can attain great speed and also maintain control on turns. The giant slalom ski is very much like the skis used by people who ski only for fun.

The proper application of wax to the bottom of skis is a very important part of Alpine racing. Some kinds of wax help skis glide more easily; other kinds help keep skis from slipping too much. Skiers must adjust the kind of wax they use to the kind of snow they will be skiing

17

Opposite: Stein Eriksen of Norway on his way to a gold medal in the 1952 giant slalom at Oslo, Norway. Metal clamps, or bindings, hold the toes and heels of his boots firmly to his skis.

on. They need to get a lot of speed as well as maintain control. If a skier uses the wrong kind of wax for the skiing conditions, he or she might be slowed down or lose control for a second or two. This is important in a sport in which the winner might take a race by only a few hundredths of a second.

Ski boots and their attachment to the skis are also important. The boots are made of a hard plastic with soft leather or foam padding inside. Boots that fit correctly give skiers control over their skis. The boot extends two or three inches above the ankle. The top part of the boot is bent forward a little, or *raked.* This makes the skiers lean forward slightly when standing on their skis. It helps the skier move forward faster.

The boots are attached to the skis by metal clamps, or *bindings.* The bindings hold the toe and heel of the boots firmly. There would be extreme danger to any skier whose ski came loose while he or she was racing at a speed of seventy miles an hour. If something does happen to make a skier fall, the bindings release from the boot. This helps prevent broken legs and ankles. In addition, a safety strap is attached to the ski behind the binding. This strap is fastened loosely around the skier's ankle. It keeps the ski with the skier if he or she falls; this prevents the danger of a ski sliding down the slope and interfering with other skiers.

Betsy Snite of the 1960 United States team speeds down the course in the tight-fitting clothing and safety helmet worn by Alpine skiers. She is using the lower part of her body for speed and control. The upper part of her body and her ski poles are being used for balance.

Skiers wear tight-fitting clothing to cut down the drag of the wind. They also wear safety helmets in case of a fall, and tinted goggles to cut down the glare from the snow. Racers carry ski poles with sharp, pointed tips and a disk or basket near the tip. Skiers use the poles to push off at the start of a race and to balance on turns. The basket keeps the pole from going too deeply into the snow and slowing down the skier. Ski racers pick equipment that gives them speed, control, and as much safety as possible.

HOW THE SKIERS SKI

Skiers in Olympic competition are masters of the sport. Through careful coaching and practice they have become expert skiers. Although there are many methods of teaching people to ski, there are some basic movements that every skier must learn.

Skiers use the lower part of the body for speed and control. They push with leg and back muscles, and control direction with knee and hip movements. The upper body is used for balance. Ski poles also help the skiers' balance.

The three important techniques skiers learn are *schussing, traversing,* and *turning.*

Schussing is skiing down a course in a straight line. It is the fastest way to ski. Expert skiers must be able to get the most speed possible and still maintain control. They balance equally on both skis and lean forward to speed up.

Opposite: Karen Budge of the United States is using a sharp, parallel turn as she maneuvers between the flags on a downhill course in 1972.

If a ski run had no turns or bends, a skier could schuss from top to bottom, but the skier might lose control by the time he or she finished a race. Therefore, a course is laid out so that the skier must ski at angles as well as straight down. Skiing at an angle to the slope is called *traversing*.

To traverse, the skier shifts his or her body weight from the center of the skis and leans to the right or left. The sharp metal edges of the skis cut into the snow and give the skier control. The skier pushes against the snow and moves in a curving line.

The most difficult move in skiing is *turning*. Turning is like traversing, only at a much sharper angle. The turns are done by taking the weight off one or both skis.

A simple turn is called a *steered* turn. The skier moves one ski so that its toe points toward the toe of the other ski and the tails of the skis move apart. The skier shifts his or her weight to the angled ski and pushes on it. The skier turns in the opposite direction of the push. The other ski is then moved in line with the angled ski. If the skier pushes the right ski, he or she moves left; if the left ski is pushed, the skier goes right. This kind of turning is used mainly on wide bends in a course. The *snowplow* and *stem* turns are forms of steered turns.

For a sharper angle the skier uses a *parallel* turn. The skis are held close to each other and are kept side by side during the turn. The skier gives a very slight jump, or "unweights" his or her skis. The knees and hips rotate, and the skis are moved to the right or left. The skier can unweight the skis because of the springiness given by the camber.

Vladimir Sabich of the United States used a variety of Alpine skiing techniques as he sped toward his goal in the men's downhill race at Grenoble, France in 1968.

Skidding is controlled because the metal edges grab the snow. The *parallel christie* is a form of this turn.

GETTING TO THE OLYMPICS

Most expert skiers learn to ski when they are very young. They take skiing lessons and practice a lot. If they have a special talent for skiing, they might start entering local races. If they do well in these races they might be asked to join the national skiing team of their country. All national ski teams have coaches who watch for talented skiers in various regions. A skier who joins a national team has taken the first step toward skiing in the Olympics.

Skiers on national teams have a chance to compete in more difficult national and international skiing contests. These races are held under the rules of the FIS, the organization that governs all skiing contests. The FIS provides two levels of competition for skiers—the Europa Cup circuit and the World Cup circuit. Skiers with little experience or those who do not ski as well as the top skiers participate in Europa Cup races. The best skiers go to World Cup races.

Each circuit includes races held at various places all over the world. Because each course is different, the skiers' records are not based on the times they take to complete a race. Instead, they earn points for the place they finish in a race. A skier who takes first place gets twenty-five points; a tenth-place finisher receives one point. The races are held from December until March. The racers who earn the most

Zeno Colo of Italy won a gold medal in 1952 for the men's downhill race.

points in the Europa Cup circuit get a chance to ski in World Cup races. The best World Cup circuit skiers are invited to go to the Olympics.

OLYMPIC COMPETITION

Medals are awarded in four Olympic Alpine skiing events. They are the *downhill, slalom, giant slalom,* and *Alpine combined* races. Each event tests different skills. The downhill is the longest race. The giant slalom is the widest. The slalom has the sharpest turns.

The winning skier is the one who completes the race in the shortest time. The course for each event is marked off by flags placed in the snow. All skiers must follow the same course. The race courses are planned around a straight line down the slope, called the *fall line.* The racers would not be able to control their run if the course went straight down, however. Turns are included in each course to force the racer to go slower at those points. In every race, the skiers must ski across, as well as down, the slope.

The races are begun when the weather is as clear as possible. One skier at a time stands at a starting gate at the top of the course. When the judge gives the signal the skier starts the race. The clock starts running as the skier goes through the gate. Skiers start about one minute apart. There are always two skiers on the course at the same time, although they are far apart. The skiers pass through an electronic beam as they finish. This stops the clock and gives them their time to a

Roland Thoeni of Italy won a bronze medal in the slalom race during the 1972 Winter Olympic Games at Sapporo, Japan.

The finish line at Sapporo, Japan.

hundredth of a second. The downhill and slalom races are run once, and the giant slalom is run twice. If something gets in the way of a skier, he or she is permitted to start the race over again after the last scheduled racer is finished.

The starting positions of racers are decided by how well they have done in other international races. This is called *seeding*. The best racers start first. The top fifteen racers are the first seed, the next fifteen are the second seed, and so on. This means that the best racers perform on the course when it is in the best condition.

Opposite: In a slalom race a skier must pass through many gates at very high speeds.

DOWNHILL The downhill race is a test of a skier's speed. The course for men is usually two to three miles long; the women's course is usually one mile long. Since the event is held on a mountain, the angle of the drop is important. The vertical drop—from top to bottom—can be 850 to 1,000 meters for men's courses and 400 to 700 meters for women's. *Control gates* are formed by a pair of rectangular flags set on two poles. All skiers must pass between the flags so that they ski the same course. The gates force the skiers to go more slowly in some spots and guide the skiers away from dangerous bumpy snow. In a race in which the skiers sometimes go more than seventy miles per hour, safety is important.

SLALOM The slalom race tests the skiers' turning ability. Its course includes many zigzags. There are many more gates in the slalom—from fifty-five to seventy-five in the men's race and forty to sixty in the women's race. The gates are marked by pairs of triangular flags set on flexible poles. Skiers must pass through every gate on the course. If a skier misses one, it means the run is not counted. Judges are placed all along the slalom course to see that the skiers go through each gate. Sometimes skiers knock down a flag, but if both skis pass through the gate, it is not counted as a miss.

Werner Mattle of Switzerland skis in an Alpine race at Sapporo, Japan in 1972.

Andrea Mead Lawrence of the United States was delighted with the gold medal she won in 1952 for the women's slalom race at Oslo, Norway

The gates are placed fairly close to one another. They can be *open gates,* placed across the fall line; *closed gates,* placed on the fall line; a tricky *combination* of open and closed gates; or *hairpin gates*—three open gates that require a wide, sharp turn. The surface of the course has both sharp drops and level surfaces. The racers must watch for gates and also watch the surfaces on which they are skiing.

The slalom is a shorter race than the downhill. In this race the vertical drop is 180 to 220 meters for men's races, and 130 to 180 meters for women's races.

The 1968 United States Alpine ski team at Grenoble, France.

Cindy Nelson of the United States receives a congratulatory kiss from a competitor at Innsbruck in 1976.

GIANT SLALOM The giant slalom is a cross between the downhill race and the slalom. It tests a skier's ability to ski across a course, or *traverse,* instead of going straight down. It has fewer gates than a slalom, about thirty in all. The course is wider than the slalom course and the gates are spaced farther apart. Skiers must pass through all the gates as fast as possible.

The gates of the giant slalom can be *open,* or across the fall line, or *blind,* with one flag almost directly behind the other. Rectangular flags of two different sizes mark the gates and tell the skier whether the gate is open or blind. The vertical drop is 250 to 500 meters in the men's races and 250 to 450 meters in the women's races. Each skier runs this course twice in competition. The other races have only single runs. The skier's best time is counted, and the fastest time wins.

COMBINED For the Alpine combined medal, points are awarded according to a skier's final standings in each race. The man and the woman skier with the best overall performance win this medal.

9

Opposite: Rosi Mittermaier of West Germany shows a glowing smile after winning three medals at Innsbruck, Austria in 1976.

SOME FAMOUS OLYMPIC ALPINE SKIERS

Skiing looks like such fun, and the skiers make it look so easy, that it is easy for people to forget the time and effort it takes to become an international ski racer. The men and women who excel at this sport must be dedicated to being the best. They ski for nine months of every year. Some even train all year round. They must travel a lot to take part in World Cup races. Many European skiers even drop out of school to ski full time.

Champion skiers seem to think it is all worthwhile. Their love for the sport makes up for their hard work. A look at a few of the women and men whose hearts and wills made them memorable skiers shows why the Olympic Alpine races are always dramatic and exciting.

WOMEN It is not often that two sisters are the talk of the Olympics. In the 1964 Games at Innsbruck, Austria, Frenchwomen **Marielle** and **Christine Goitschel** kept the winnings "all in the family." They each earned a gold and a silver medal in the competitions.

Christine, the older sister, was a smooth, exact skier. Marielle was athletic and seemed to attack a course. Their different skiing styles helped them in the events they won. Christine won her gold in the slalom. She cut through the gates perfectly. Marielle's drive to be a winner helped her in this race, too. She took the second-place silver

IBM

Opposite: Part of the slalom course at Grenoble, France in the 1968 Winter Games.

medal. In the giant slalom race two days later, Marielle pushed her way to a gold medal, while Christine skied elegantly to a silver-medal finish. Four years later at Grenoble, France, Marielle added to the family collection when she took a gold medal for the slalom in the 1968 Olympics. The two sisters had accomplished something unique, a success that will be hard to repeat.

Nancy Greene of Canada was a skier who had to be polished before she shone. She did not begin to enter competitions until she was fourteen, but only two years later she skied in the 1960 Olympics. Although she had done well in many international races, she had no success in either the 1960 or 1964 Olympics.

Then Greene began to show what a wonderful skier she was. She improved consistently after the 1964 Games, winning race after race. In 1967 the first World Cup was held. That year Greene became the first woman to win the World Cup championship, and in 1968 she made her dream of Olympic gold come true. She took a silver medal in the slalom and a gold in the giant slalom at Grenoble, France. That same year she won a second World Cup championship. Her eight-year wait for success in the Olympics had finally paid off. Her consistency made her one of skiing's most admired women.

Opposite: Barbara Cochran of the United States on her way to a gold medal for the slalom race at Sapporo, Japan in 1972.

A "duel" between a Swiss and an Austrian skier brought big surprises at the 1972 Games at Sapporo, Japan. **Annamarie Pröll** of Austria was favored to win the downhill race. She was an excellent racer, and the only woman to have won three World Cup championships. Pröll knew that everyone thought she would win. Perhaps that made her nervous. To the great surprise of all, Pröll lost the gold medal to **Marie-Therese Nadig** of Switzerland. Nadig, only seventeen years old, was the youngest skier to win a gold medal in the downhill. She was an almost unknown skier. The only other title she had won was the Swiss Junior championship.

Pröll and Nadig faced each other again in the giant slalom. Pröll seemed to have regained her confidence after coming in second in the downhill. Nadig ambushed her again, however, and won a second gold medal.

Sapporo was the scene of another surprising race. **Barbara Cochran** was a United States skier from Vermont. Her whole family was involved in skiing. Her father was her coach, and a brother and a sister also skied in Olympic competitions. In 1972 Cochran won a gold medal in the slalom—by only *two-hundredths* of a second! It was the narrowest winning margin a skier had ever had—and it was only the third gold medal the United States women's teams had won in Olympic history. Yes, surprising was the word for Sapporo.

5

Opposite: Rosi Mittermaier of West Germany won two gold medals at Innsbruck, Austria in the 1976 Winter Olympic Games. Her first gold was awarded for the downhill race and the second for the slalom race.

Rosi Mittermaier of West Germany, twenty-five years old, echoed Nadig's success in the 1976 Games at Innsbruck, Austria. Mittermaier came very close to winning all three Alpine events—something accomplished only twice before in Olympic history, and both of those times by men. Mittermaier was a ten-year veteran of international racing as she came to the 1976 Games. She took her first gold medal in the downhill race, defeating an Austrian favorite, **Brigitte Totschnig.** If Mittermaier and Totschnig had run their races side by side, Mittermaier would have won by fifteen yards. Mittermaier was particularly proud of her first victory. Her mother was watching her race a downhill for the first time. So were almost every man, woman, and child from Reit im Winkel, her small hometown in West Germany. Mittermaier took a second gold medal in the slalom race. The whole world was cheering her on during the giant slalom. But she made a mistake on the lower part of the course, and came in second. Mittermaier was delighted with her accomplishments, victories that she had never expected. Others were also delighted with her marvelous skiing. Three hours after her downhill rush, a crowd was still gathered outside her hotel. They chanted "Rosie! Rosie! Rosie!"—calling for her to make just one more appearance on her hotel balcony.

Anton "Toni" Sailer of Austria, nicknamed the "Black Angel" because of his dark-haired good looks, shows his gold medal style during the 1956 downhill race at Cortina, Italy.

MEN The man probably considered the best Alpine skier of all time was **Anton "Toni" Sailer** of Austria. He had started skiing when he was two, and was competing in races before he was ten. When he was fourteen he won the Austrian Junior championship, which he kept for the next three years. He broke his leg in 1952, however, and it was four years before he was able to get into the swing of things again. His skiing constantly improved, and he won five important international races that led up to the Olympics. By the time the 1956 Games were held at Cortina, Italy, Sailer was ready to make Olympic history.

Sailer was nicknamed the "Black Angel" by the Austrians because of his dark-haired good looks. This angel flew to his first victory in the downhill race. He then followed with gold medals in the slalom and the giant slalom. For the first time in the Olympics a skier had won gold medals in all three Alpine events. His feat was made even more important because he beat his nearest rivals by many seconds. Sailer is still one of Austria's most popular athletes, and was the coach of the 1976 Austrian Olympic team.

United States men's Alpine teams have never produced an Olympic gold medalist. In recent times only **Billy Kidd** of Vermont came even close to realizing a dream of a gold medal. He was one of amateur skiing's top racers from 1964 to 1970 on the World Cup circuit. A relaxed skier who understood the theories of skiing, Kidd was the only male United States skier to win a World Cup championship. He was narrowly beaten in the 1964 Olympic slalom race, and brought home a

Jean-Claude Killy of France flashes a delighted smile at Grenoble, France in 1968. Killy won three gold medals that year—one for each Alpine event.

Jean-Claude Killy in action.

silver medal. An injured ankle kept him from victory in the 1968 Games, leaving the way clear for a French skier to sweep to victory.

Jean-Claude Killy was raised in the skiing town of Val d'Isere, France, the same town that had produced the remarkable Goitschel sisters. He began skiing when he was seven, and by the time he was sixteen he was skiing in World Cup events. Before the 1968 Olympics at Grenoble, France, he had won almost every honor on the World Cup circuit. In 1968 he crowned his career by repeating Toni Sailer's achievement of winning three gold Olympic medals.

Killy took his first medal in the downhill, winning by only eight-hundredths of a second. A second gold was won in the giant slalom. Killy was then declared the winner of the slalom race. An Austrian skier, Karl Schranz, had a better time than Killy, but Schranz was disqualified. Those who were angry over Schranz's loss pointed out that Killy was not as good as Toni Sailer, because Killy's margins of victory were much smaller than Sailer's. However, Killy had ended his career as an amateur with honor, in spite of the dispute over his third gold medal.

Steve Mahre

Phil Mahre

Pete Patterson

Heidi Preuss

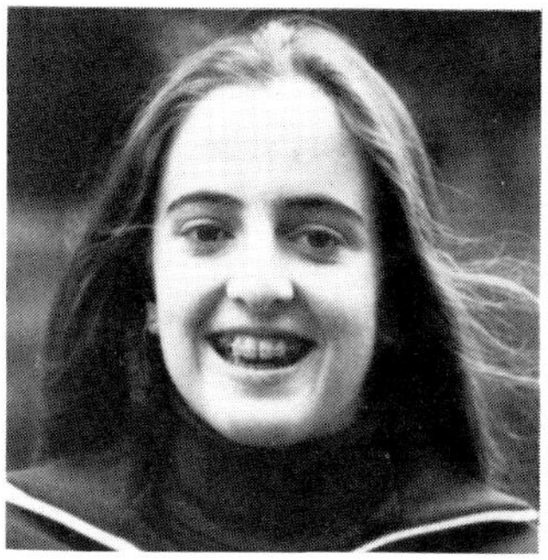

Tamara McKinney

Viki Fleckenstein

Abbi Fisher

Becky Dorsey

Some members of the United States 1980 Olympic Alpine ski team.

Christin Cooper

Cindy Nelson

Karl Schranz, even though he never won a gold medal at the Olympics, was one of the best Austrian skiers in history. He competed in international races for seventeen years. That is a very long career for an amateur skier. Schranz was able to ski for such a long time because he learned to adapt his skiing style to new kinds of equipment and techniques. He was very serious about his skiing and felt he was a loser if he did not take first place in every race he skied. He won every international race and honor at least once in his career. His only disappointment was in the Olympics.

In the 1968 Olympics at Grenoble, France, Schranz thought he had won a gold medal in the slalom. During his first run he missed two gates, but said that someone had run out on the course in front of him and distracted him. He was allowed to rerun the race, and posted a winning time. Later, however, the judges decided that he should have been disqualified in the first run. As a result, he had not been entitled to a second run, and that new time was not allowed to stand. The gold medal was given to Jean-Claude Killy.

Schranz was unhappy about losing in 1968, but he was even more disappointed in 1972. He was not allowed to ski in the Olympics at Sapporo, Japan that year. The International Olympic Committee (IOC) had been upset that their "amateur" skiers were earning money

Alain Navillod of France literally "jumps" through the gates during a 1976 race at Innsbruck, Austria.

from ski equipment makers. Many skiers "advertised" equipment by displaying the brand names when they were photographed for newspapers and magazines. The skiers used the money to pay for their training and travel expenses. The IOC thought this was wrong. The committee felt that Karl Schranz had been the worst offender and they disqualified him from the Olympics. He was the only skier punished this way, even though other skiers were equally guilty. The Austrian skiers were furious. They almost did not ski in the 1972 Games. But Schranz, a man who loved skiing more than anything else, convinced the rest of his team to compete. His devotion to his sport won over his disappointment.

Because of their troubles in the 1972 Olympics, the Austrians were particularly delighted when one of their teammates, **Franz Klammer,** won a gold medal at the 1976 Olympics. Klammer's nickname was "The Astronaut." He had rocketed to eight straight victories in World Cup downhill races before the 1976 Games at Innsbruck, Austria.

In the 1976 Olympic downhill, Klammer skied last in the first seeding; this meant he was the fifteenth man to go down the slope. By the time he skied, the course was icy and rough. Klammer wanted desperately to win. This showed in the way he skied his race. He took chances and shot down the slope at a great speed, in spite of the icy conditions. The former farm boy from Austria did it. Klammer won the race by .33 seconds. Austria again had a skier to be proud of, and the whole world had an athlete to admire.

The United States Olympic Alpine ski team for 1980.

OLYMPIC GOLD MEDALISTS

Alpine Skiing

Men

DOWNHILL

Year	Name	Country
1948	Henri Oreiller	France
1952	Zeno Colo	Italy
1956	Anton Sailer	Austria
1960	Jean Vuarnet	France
1964	Egon Zimmermann	Austria
1968	Jean Claude Killy	France
1972	Bernhard Russi	Switzerland
1976	Franz Klammer	Austria

SLALOM

Year	Name	Country
1948	Edy Reinalter	Switzerland
1952	Othmar Schneider	Austria
1956	Anton Sailer	Austria
1960	Ernst Hinterseer	Austria
1964	Josef Stiegler	Austria
1968	Jean Claude Killy	France
1972	Francesco Fernandez Ochoa	Spain
1976	Piero Gros	Italy

GIANT SLALOM

Year	Name	Country
1952	Stein Eriksen	Norway
1956	Anton Sailer	Austria
1960	Roger Staub	Switzerland
1964	Francois Boulieu	France
1968	Jean Claude Killy	France
1972	Gustavo Thoeni	Italy
1976	Heini Hemmi	Switzerland

OLYMPIC GOLD MEDALISTS

Alpine Skiing
Women

DOWNHILL

Year	Name	Country
1948	Hedy Schlunegger	Switzerland
1952	Gertrud Jochum-Beiser	Austria
1956	Madeline Berthod	Switzerland
1960	Heidi Biebl	Germany
1964	Christl Haas	Austria
1968	Olga Pall	Austria
1972	Marie-Therese Nadig	Switzerland
1976	Rosi Mittermaier	West Germany

SLALOM

Year	Name	Country
1948	Gretchen Fraser	United States
1952	Andrea Mead Lawrence	United States
1956	Rene Colliaird	Switzerland
1960	Anne Heggtveit	Canada
1964	Christine Goitschel	France
1968	Marielle Goitschel	France
1972	Barbara Cochran	United States
1976	Rosi Mittermaier	West Germany

GIANT SLALOM

Year	Name	Country
1952	Andrea Mead Lawrence	United States
1956	Ossi Reichert	Germany
1960	Yvonne Ruegg	Switzerland
1964	Marielle Goitschel	France
1968	Nancy Greene	Canada
1972	Marie-Therese Nadig	Switzerland
1976	Kathy Kreiner	Canada